Alfred's Basic Guitar Method 3

Completely revised and edited, including up-to-the-minute modern guitar techniques such as hammer-ons, pull-offs, slides, grace notes, string bending or choking, diminished and augmented chords, dance rhythms, and much more.

Contents

What You Should Know Before Starting this Book	2
Chord Exercises	5
Sixteenth Notes	6
Mixin' It Up	6
The Happy Sailor	7
Variations on a Square Dance Tune	7
Etude in D	7
Introducing Arpeggios	8
East Side, West Side	8
The Man on the Flying Trapeze	8
Scarborough Fair (Duet)	9
The Doo-Wop Ballad	10
My Angel Baby (Duet)	11
The Key of A Major	12
Tunes That Teach Technic No. 1	13
Scale Etude in A Major	13
Arpeggio Etude	13
Hard, Ain't It Hard	14
Hail, Hail, The Gang's All Here	14
Sixteenth Note Studies in A Major	15
Hammer-ons	16
John Hardy	17
Old Blue	17
Calypso	18
Hey Lolly Lolly	19
The Sloop "John B."	19
The Key of D Minor	20
Sicilian Tarantella	21
Sixteenth Notes and 6/8 Time	22
The House of the Rising Sun (Duet)	23
The Key of E Major	24
Finger Exercise in E	25
The Blue Tail Fly	25
Using Passing Notes in the Bass	26
Diminished Chords	28
You Tell Me Your Dream	29
Pull-offs	30
Country Dance	31
Blues in A	31
The Polka (Duet)	32
Grace Notes	34
Amazing Grace Notes	34
Colonel Bogey	35
Augmented Chords	36
Slides and How To Play Them	38
Slidin' Around (Duet)	39
Tunes That Teach Technic No. 2	40
Devil's Dream Hornpipe	40
Our Katie	40
Abide With Me (Duet)	41
Beguine	42
Guitarra Romana (Duet)	42
Bends or Chokes	44
Bending the Blues	45
Pistol Pete	45
Counterpoint	46
Simple Melody (Trio)	46
Tunes That Teach Technic No. 3	48
Onyx Club Hop	48
Just Lopin' Along	48
Jingle for a Sunny Day	48

Copyright © MCMXCIII by Alfred Publishing Co., Inc.   All Rights Reserved.   Printed in U.S.A.

Guitar photo courtesy of the Martin Guitar Company

Book production and music engraving: Bruce Goldes

What You Should Know Before Starting this Book

If you have completed Books 1 and 2 of Alfred's Basic Guitar Method (or other equivalent books), you will know the following about playing single notes on the guitar. Make sure you can play these exercises perfectly before continuing.

Key of C, basic note values

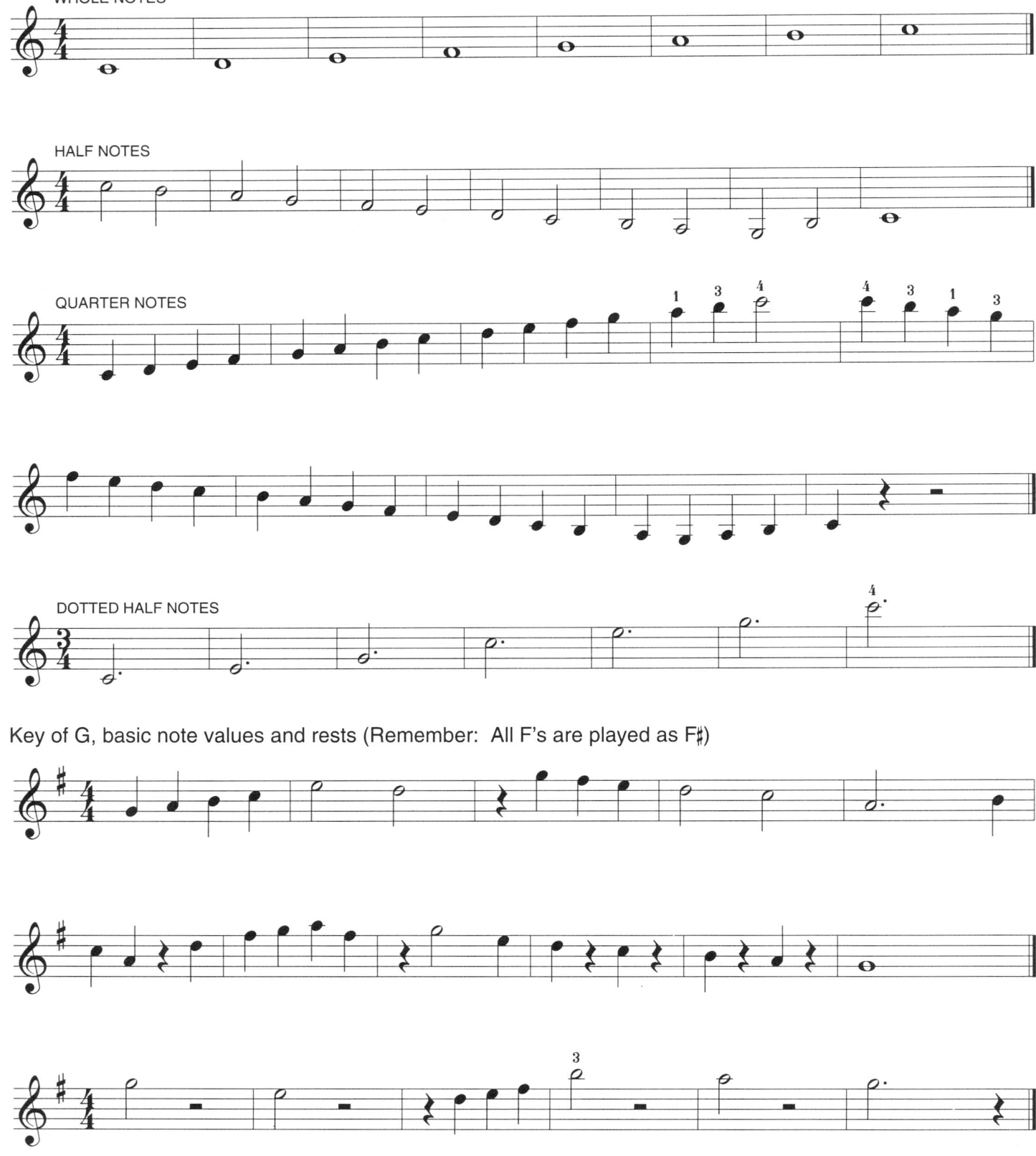

Key of G, basic note values and rests (Remember: All F's are played as F#)

Key of F, 8th notes and 8th rests (Remember: All B's are played as B♭)

Key of A minor, dotted quarter notes

Fragment from *Hungarian Dance*

Franz Liszt

Key of E minor, dotted eighths and sixteenths (all F's are played as F♯)

Triplets

High notes in Key of D (F's and C's are played as F♯ and C♯)

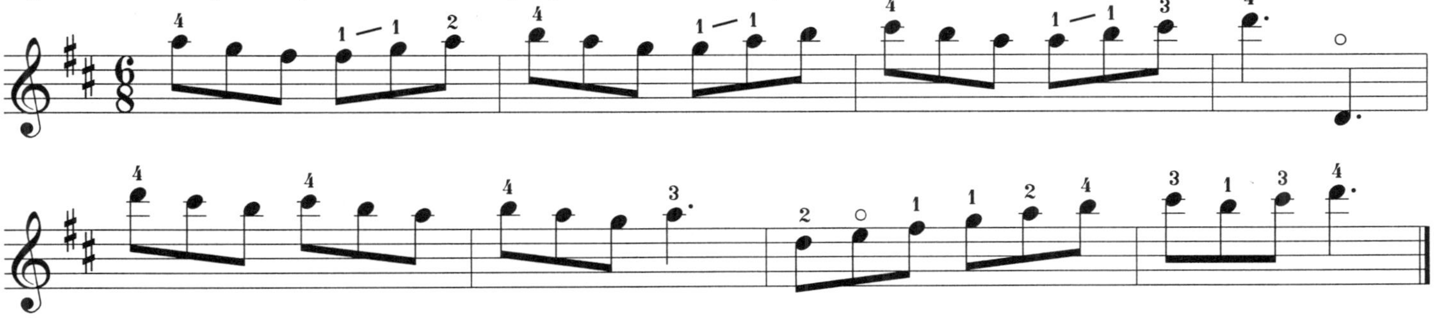

Syncopation

Before continuing further, make sure you know the following chords, their primary bass notes (roots) and alternate bass notes. You should also be able to recognize the chords when they are written out in notes.

Major Chords

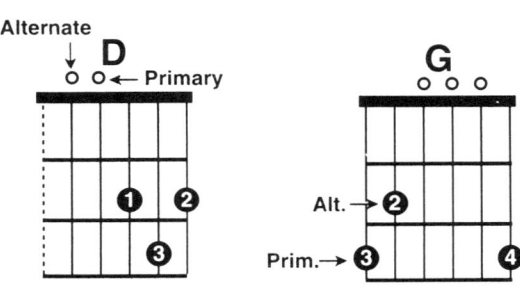 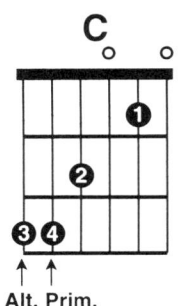 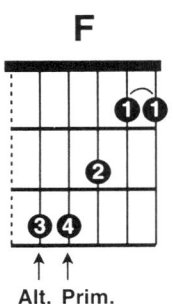 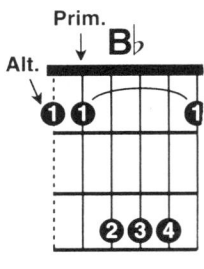

Minor Chords

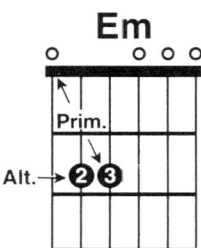 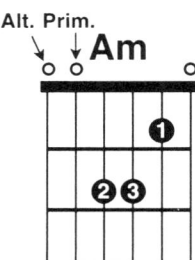 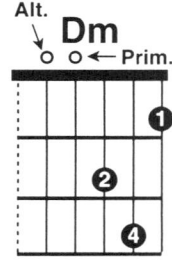

Seventh Chords

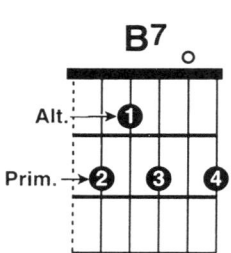 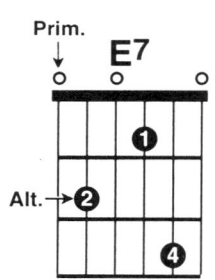 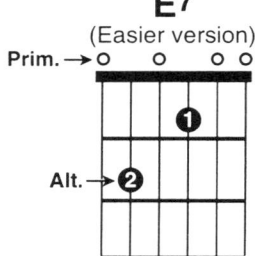 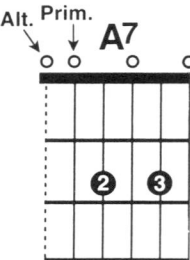

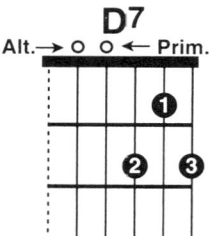 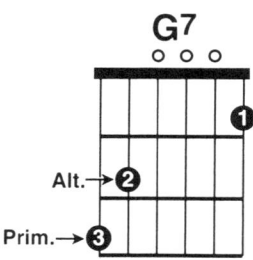 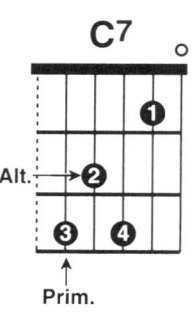

Chord Exercises

Make sure you can play the following chord exercises without missing a beat:

Key of C Major

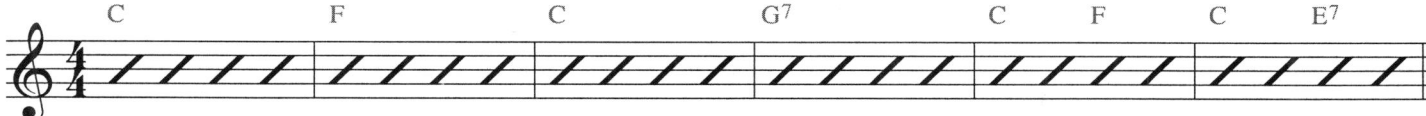

Key of A Minor

Key of F Major

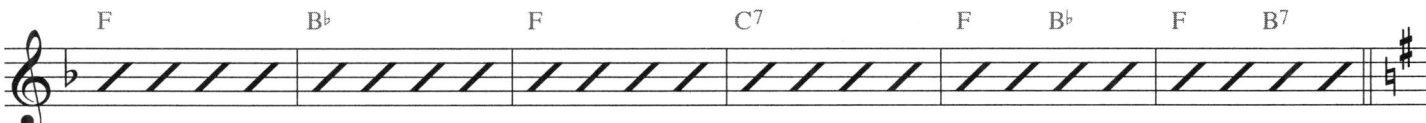

Key of E Minor

Key of G Major

Key of D Major

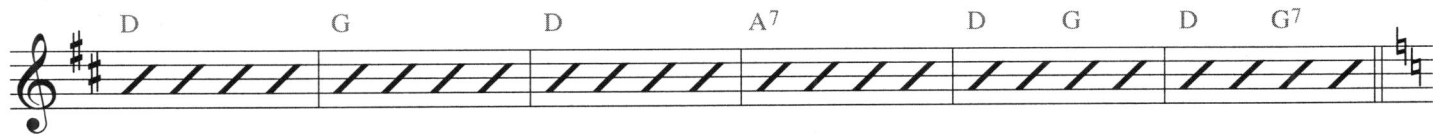

Key of C Major

𝄎 MEANS REPEAT PREVIOUS MEASURE

Key of G Major

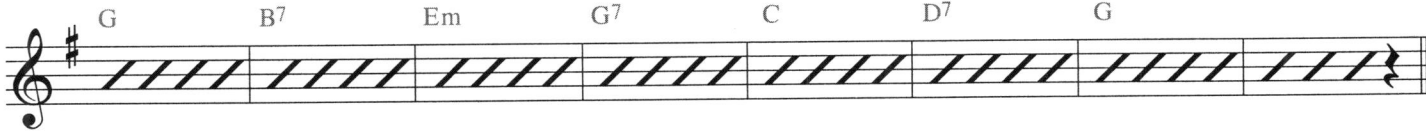

The above exercises can be played either:
1. Strumming once for each / (slash)
2. Substituting a primary bass note for the 1st beat of each measure
3. Substituting a primary bass note for the 1st beat of each measure and an alternate bass note for the 3rd beat of each measure.

Sixteenth Notes

Sixteenth notes are black notes with two flags added to the stems ♪ or ♪

Generally when two or more sixteenth notes are played, they are joined with two beams:

Sixteenth notes are played four to a beat, twice as fast as eighth notes and four times as fast as quarter notes. Use alternate picking when playing sixteenth notes.

4 quarter notes = 8 eighth notes = 16 sixteenth notes

In 2/4 time

In 3/4 time

Mixin' It Up

The pattern of an eighth note followed by two sixteenth notes is very common. The following song illustrates it. Watch the picking carefully.

The Happy Sailor

The rhythm of two sixteenth notes followed by an eighth note is also fairly common. Again, watch your picking carefully.

Variations on a Square Dance Tune

Etude in D

Introducing Arpeggios

When the notes of a chord are played in succession it is an ARPEGGIO.

Scarborough Fair

This beautiful English folk song was a big hit for Simon and Garfunkel in the '60s. It is arranged here as a duet, and the student should learn both parts. Keep the arpeggios flowing smoothly in the second part with fingers held down as long as possible.

The Doo-Wop Ballad

In the 1950s a style of rock and roll ballad called "doo-wop" became very popular. This type of song featured many long held notes sung over an accompaniment of triplets, played either as chords or arpeggios. Here are a few samples of each.

Key of C (Chords)

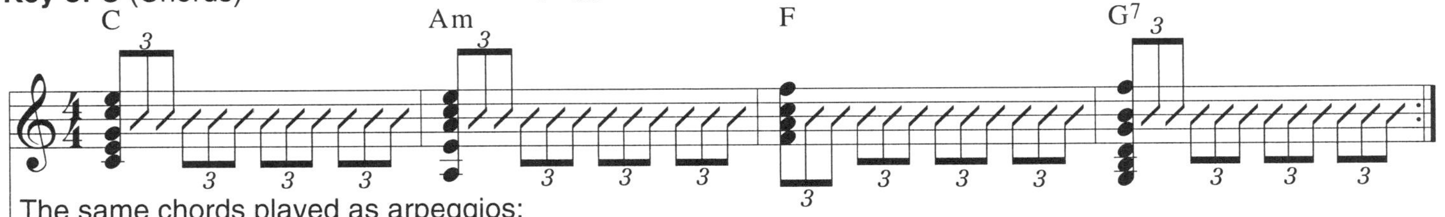

The same chords played as arpeggios:

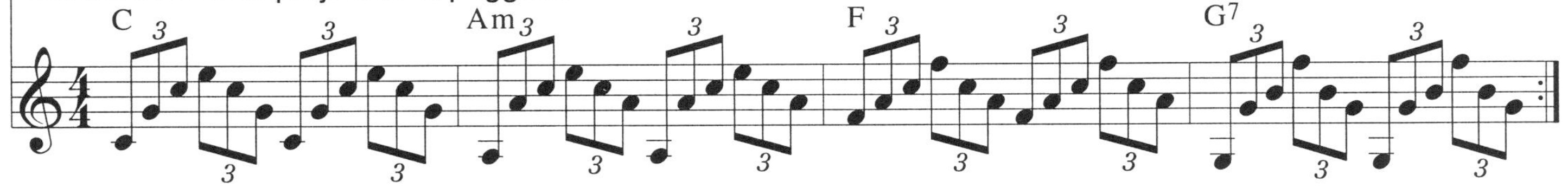

Important: Hold fingers down for the above arpeggios as long as possible

Key of G (Chords)

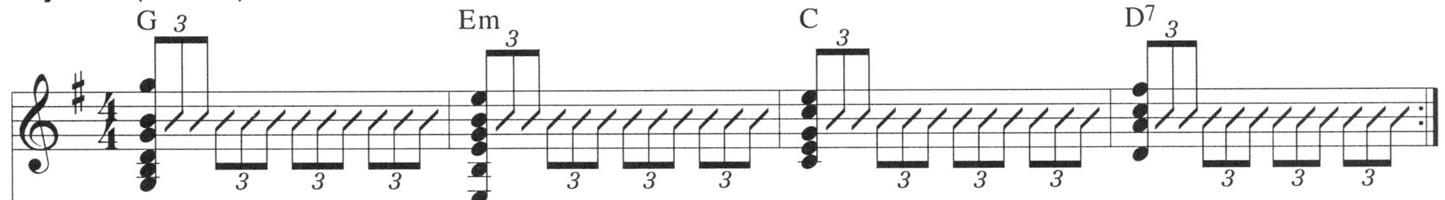

Arpeggios:

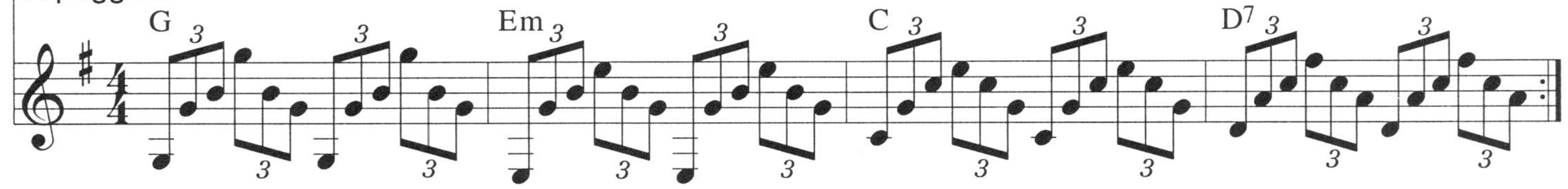

Key of C Chords, with bass notes

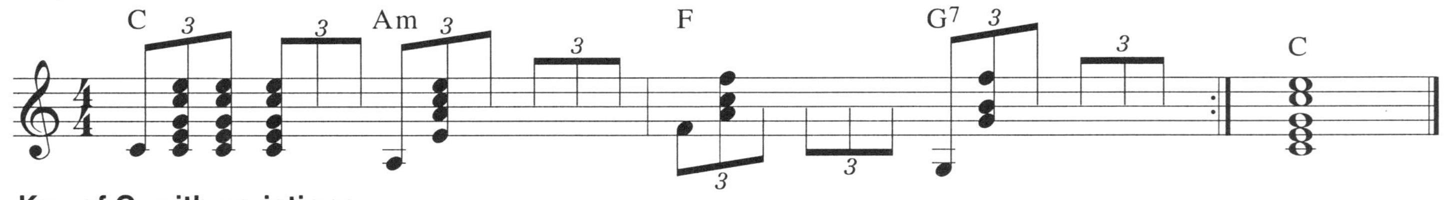

Key of C, with variations

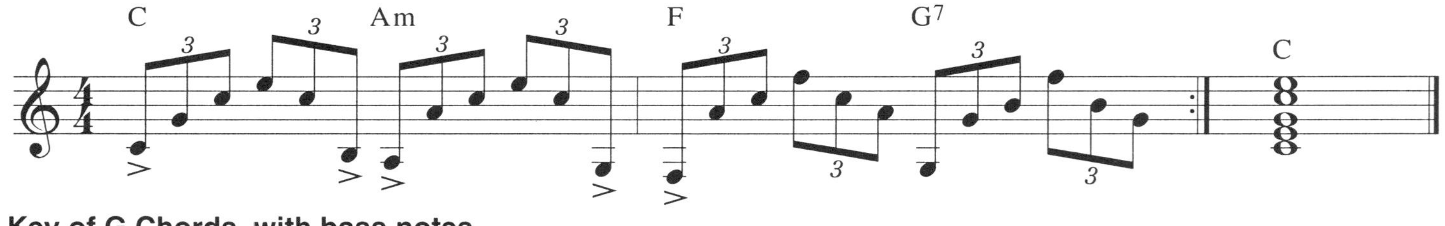

Key of G Chords, with bass notes

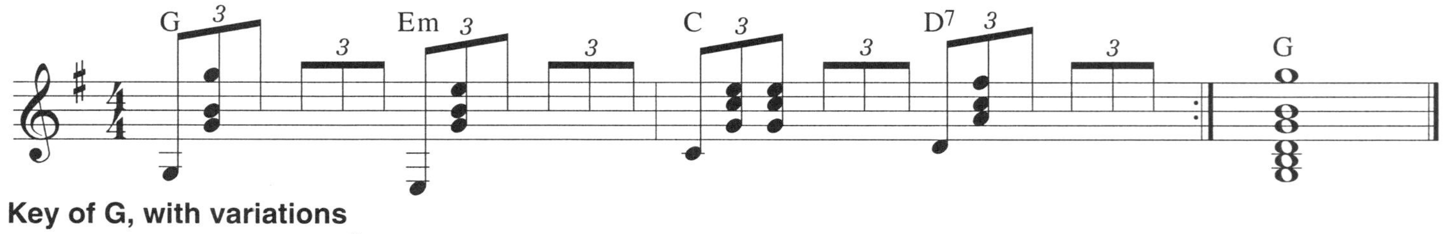

Key of G, with variations

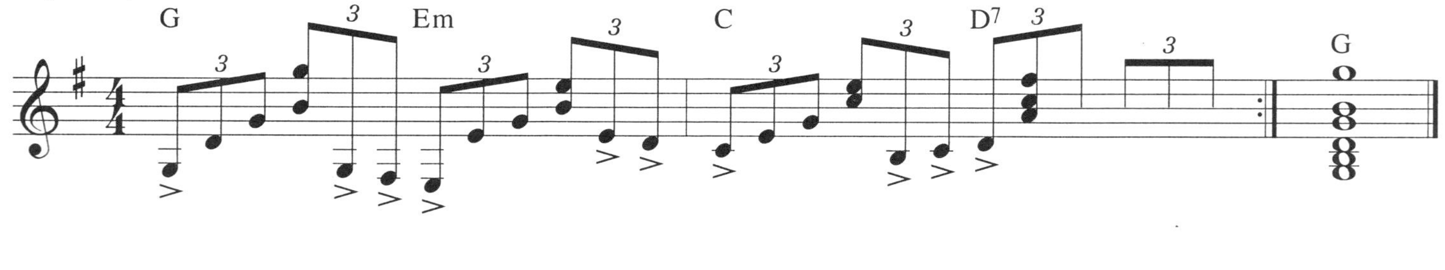

Here is a song written in '50s "doo-wop" style. Learn the melody and arpeggio-style accompaniment.

My Angel Baby

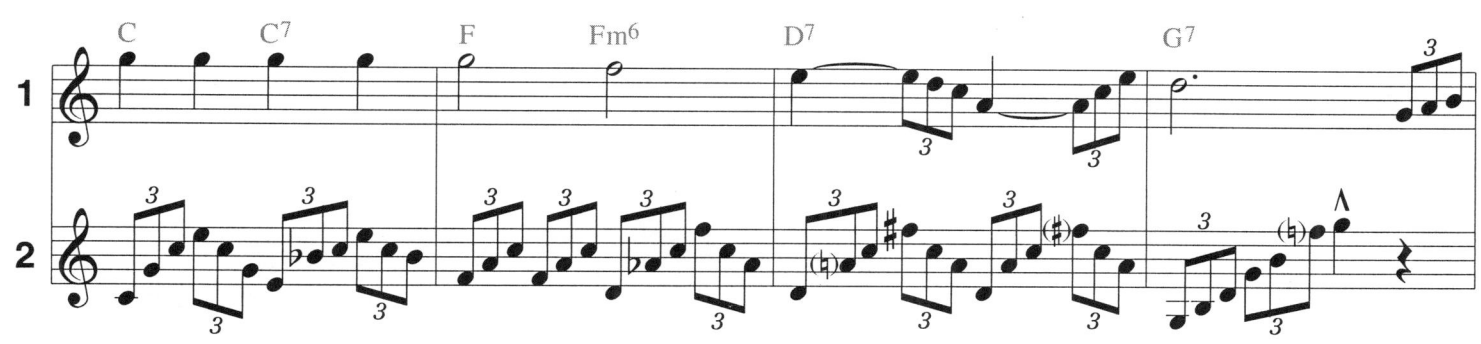
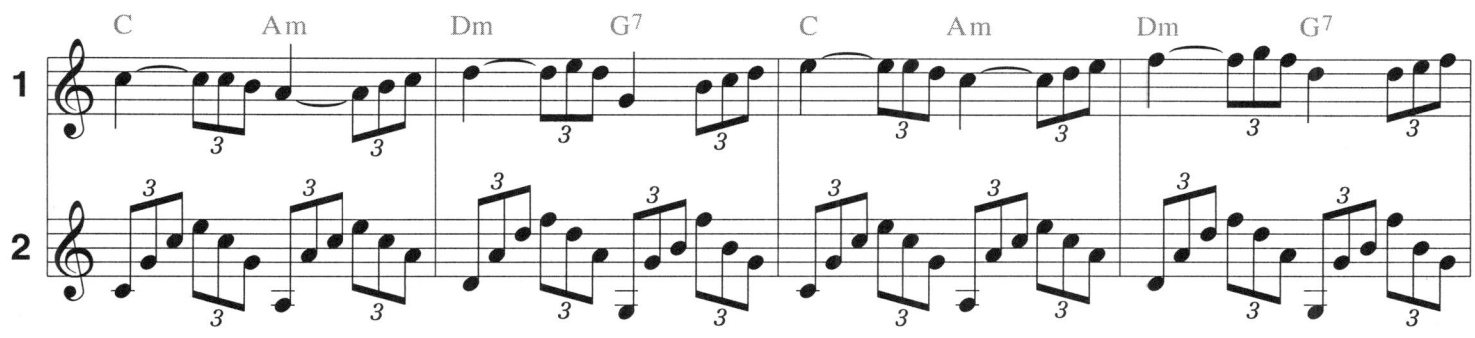
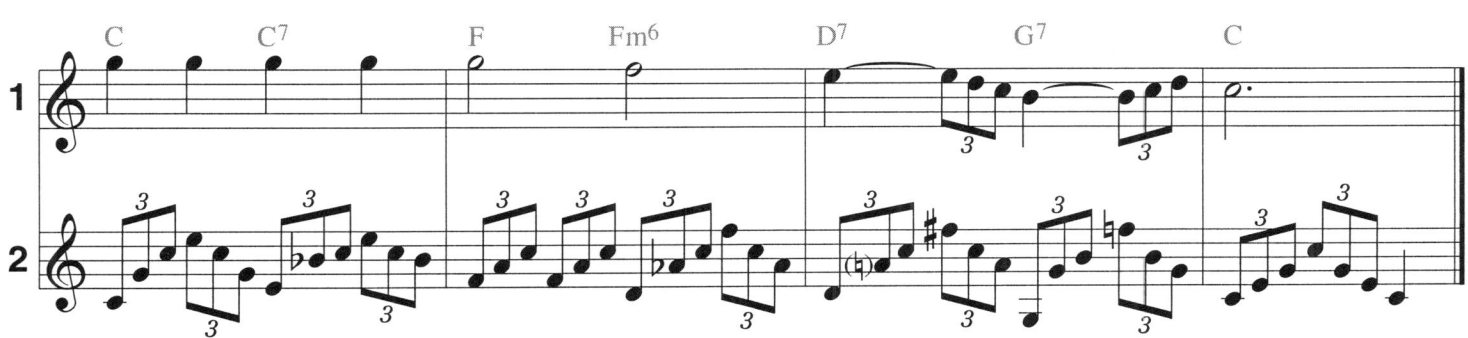

The Key of A Major

The key signature of three sharps indicates the key of A major. All F's are played as F#, all C's are played as C#, and all G's are played as G# unless otherwise indicated by a natural sign.

When learning the two-octave A major scale below, follow the fingering carefully. Like all scales, this one should be practiced daily.

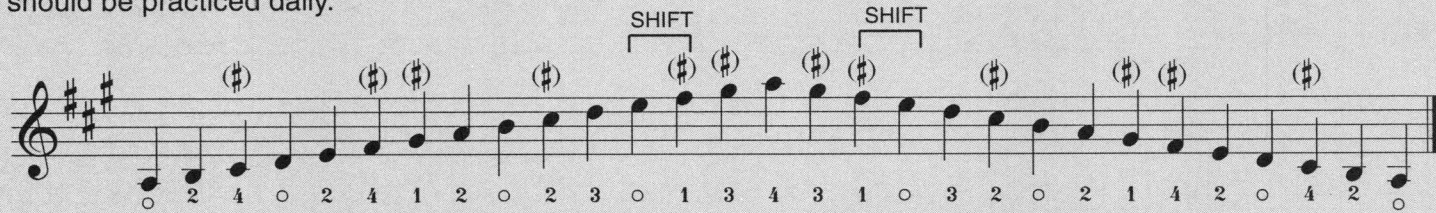

The Three Principal Chords in A with Bass Notes

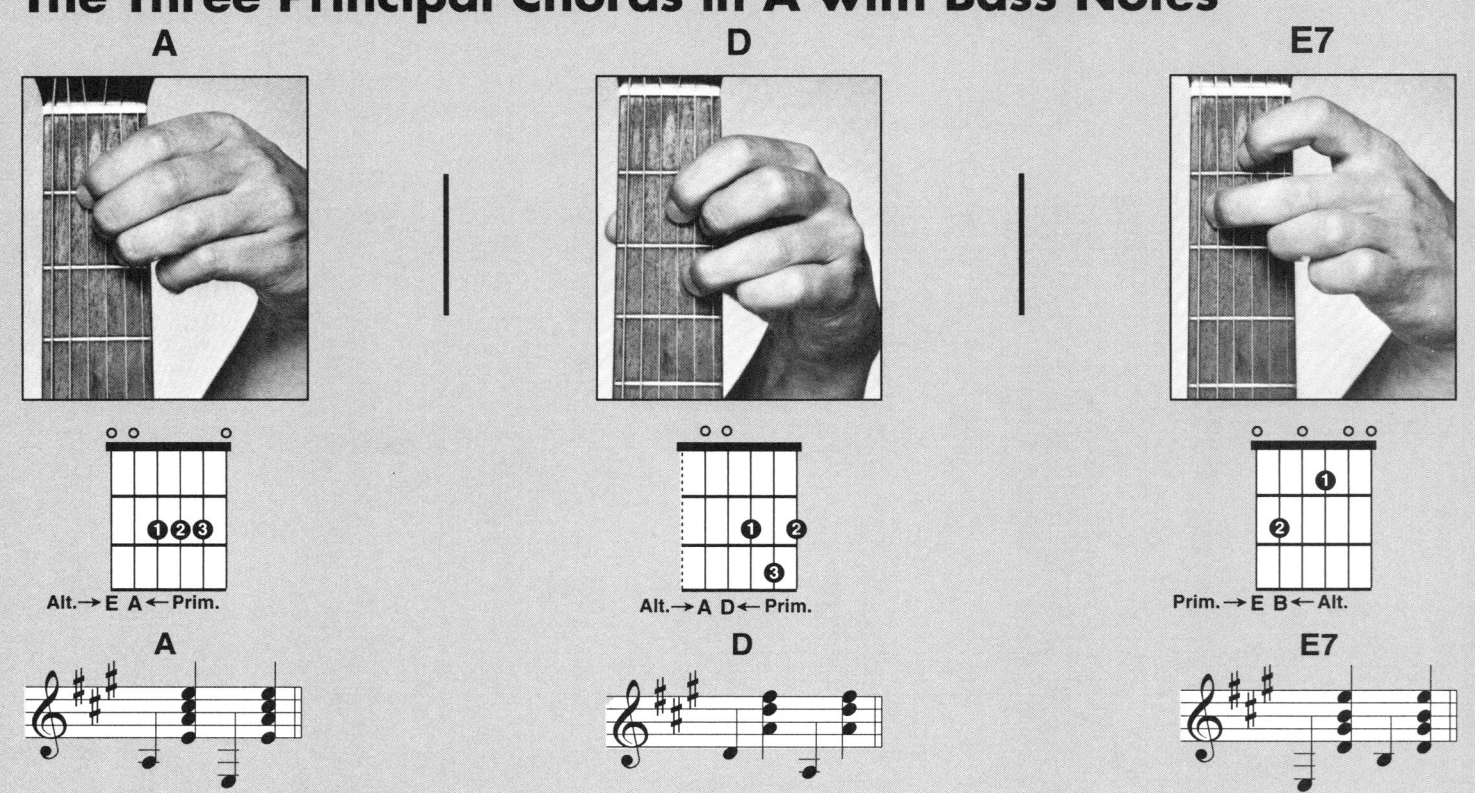

Accompaniments in A Major

Arpeggio Style

Tunes That Teach Technic No. 1

Scale Etude in A Major

Arpeggio Etude

HOLD FINGERS IN PLACE AS LONG AS POSSIBLE

Hard, Ain't It Hard

Traditional

Bright country tempo

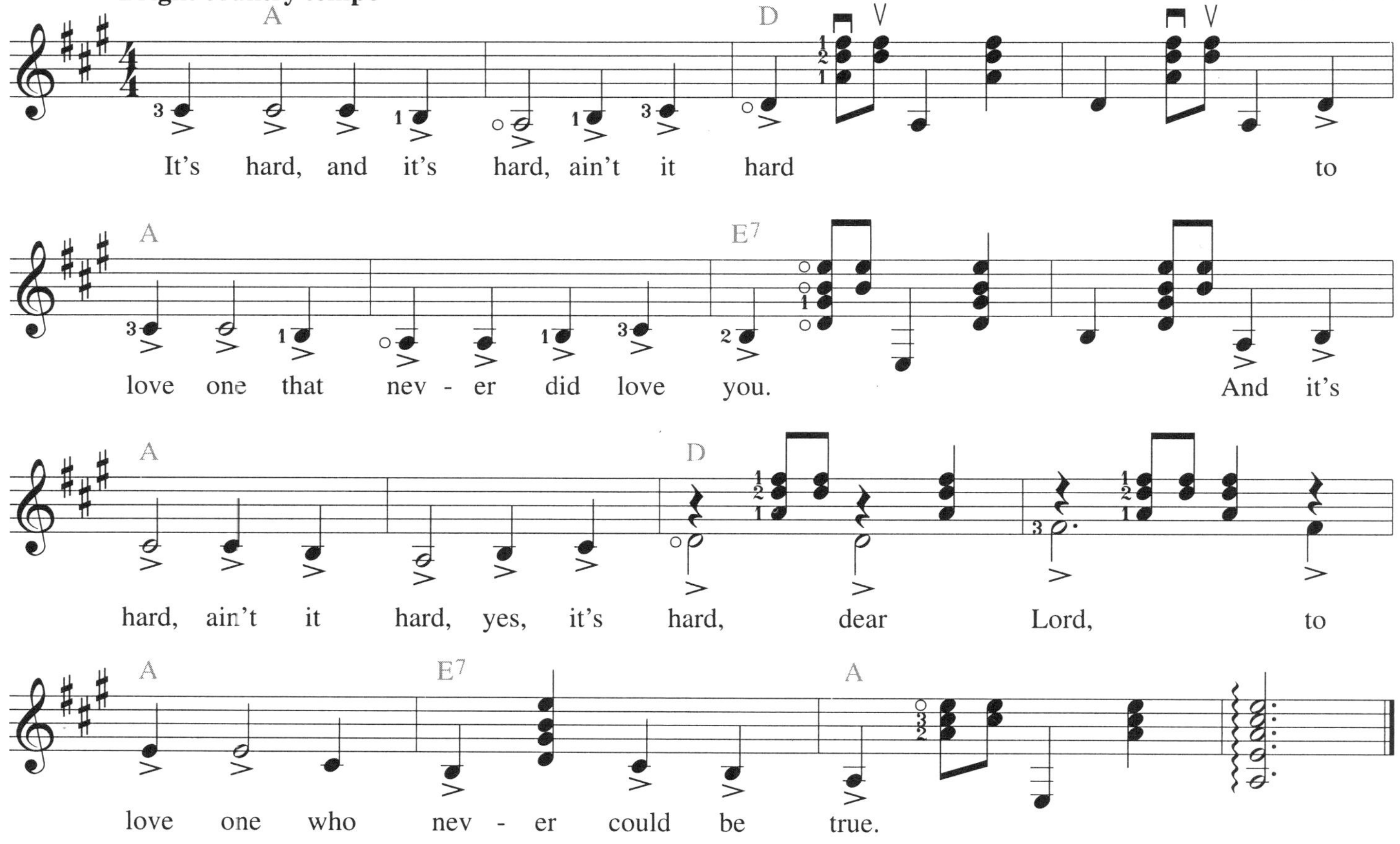
A D A E7 A D A E7 A
It's hard, and it's hard, ain't it hard to
love one that never did love you. And it's
hard, ain't it hard, yes, it's hard, dear Lord, to
love one who never could be true.

Hail, Hail, The Gang's All Here

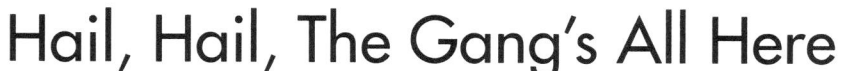

Words: Anon.

Music: Sir Arthur Sullivan

Like a march, in 2 (♩. = 1 beat)

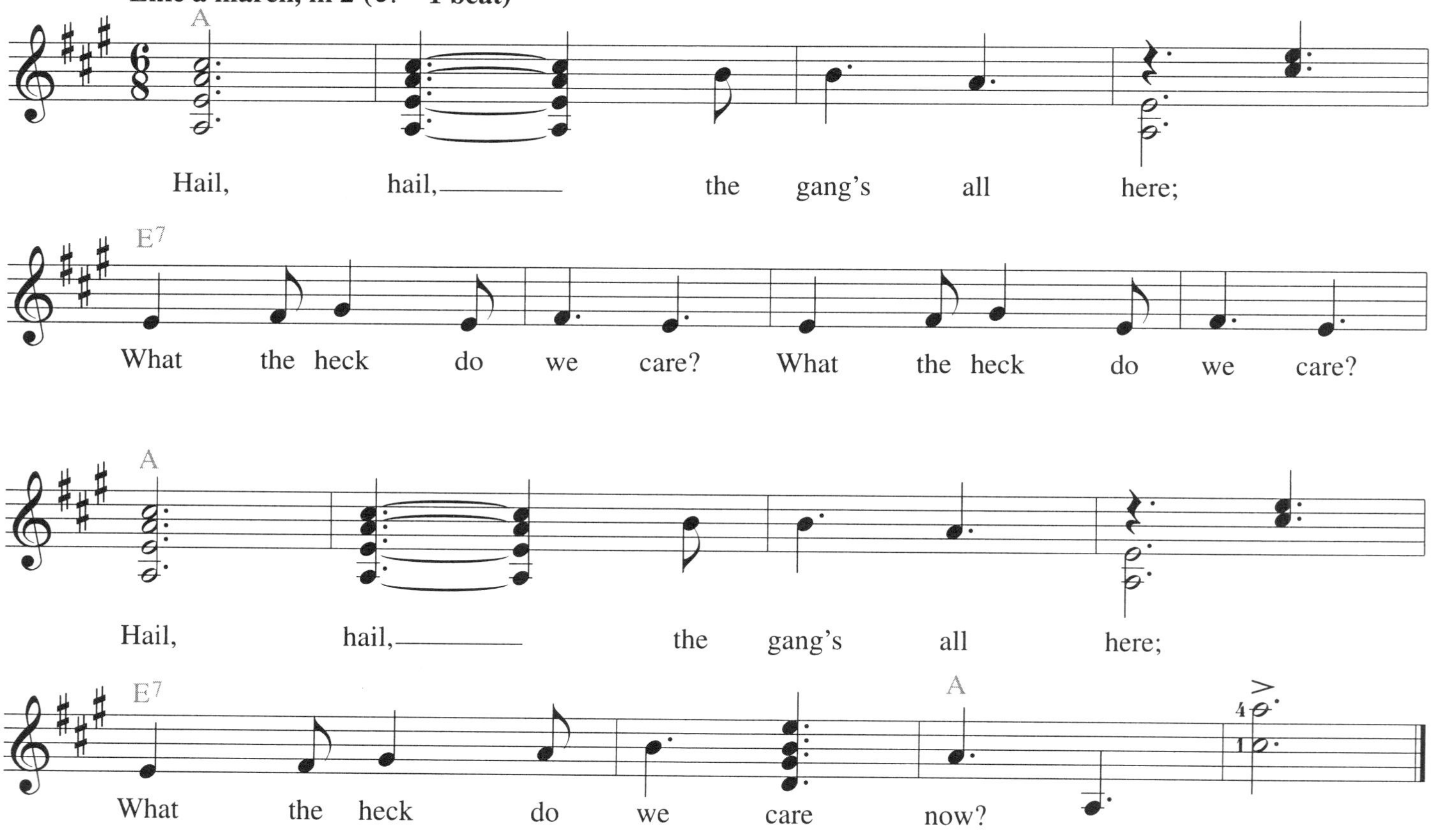
A E7 A E7 A
Hail, hail, the gang's all here;
What the heck do we care? What the heck do we care?
Hail, hail, the gang's all here;
What the heck do we care now?

Sixteenth Note Studies in A Major

Hammer-ons

The hammer-on effect is very common in today's music, especially in rock, heavy metal, country, blues and jazz. Every guitarist should be able to play this exciting technique. Hammer-on means playing a note by bringing a left-hand finger down hard enough to sound the note.

A hammer-on to a *fingered* string is done like this:

1. Start with the fingered note, the E on the 4th string, 2nd fret.
2. Strike the string with the pick while keeping the 1st finger firmly in place.

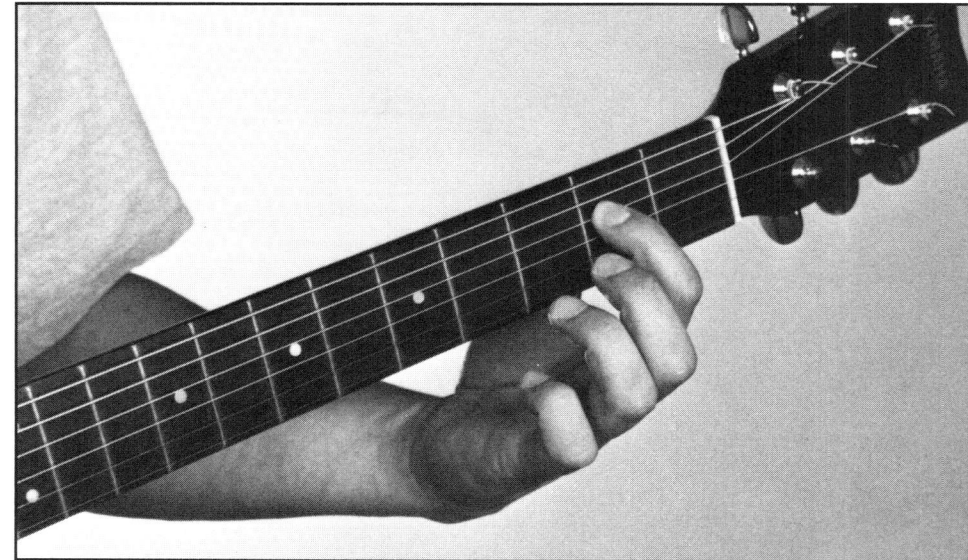

3. Then hammer the 2nd finger down hard and fast. The F will sound.

In musical notation, this is written:

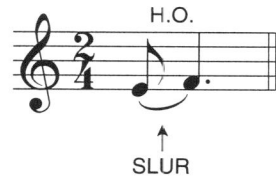

The curved line between the E and the F is called a slur and means that the F is not picked. The initials "H.O." above the staff stand for hammer-on. (Not all publications use this abbreviation.)

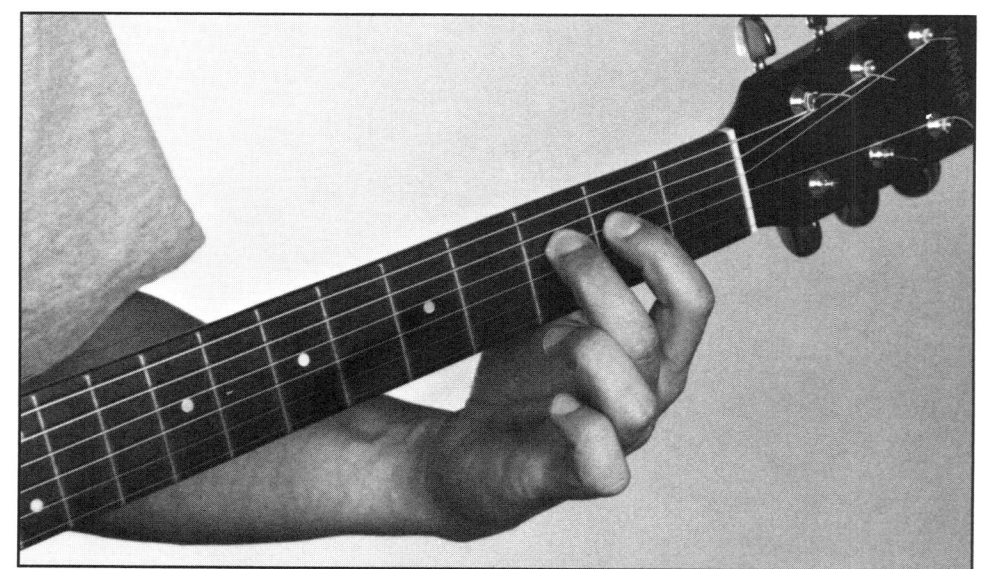

A hammer-on to an *open* string is done like this:

1. Strike the open A string with the pick.
2. Bring the 2nd finger down on the A string, 2nd fret, with a fast, hard, hammering motion and keep it there.
3. The note B will sound without picking the string a second time.

Here it is in music notation: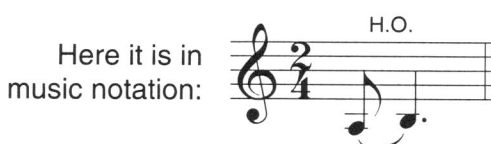

"John Hardy" and "Old Blue" are written in cut time (also called *alla breve*). The symbol for this is ₵, which means that the music is counted two beats to a measure. Every note value is cut by half: whole notes get two beats, half notes one beat, quarter notes a half beat each and so on.

Calypso

Calypso is Caribbean music of West African derivation. It was originally a means of social commentary sung over a rhythmic background and is a direct ancestor of today's rap music. A more Americanized type of calypso became popular in the '50s through the recordings of Harry Belafonte and others. These records featured the guitar in a prominent rhythmic role, but not usually as a solo instrument. Since most calypso songs use only a few chords, students can learn to play calypso music by mastering the rhythm pattern, called a strum.

To start, play the following strum:
(follow the picking carefully)

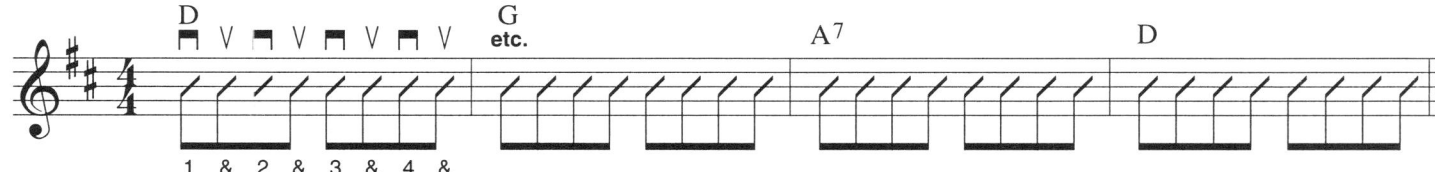

Now omit the beat played at 3

As you can see, the tricky part is leaving out the 3rd beat and playing the two up-picks in a row.

Here are some typical calypso chord progressions. Practice them until you can play them without missing a beat. Then try the song on the next page.

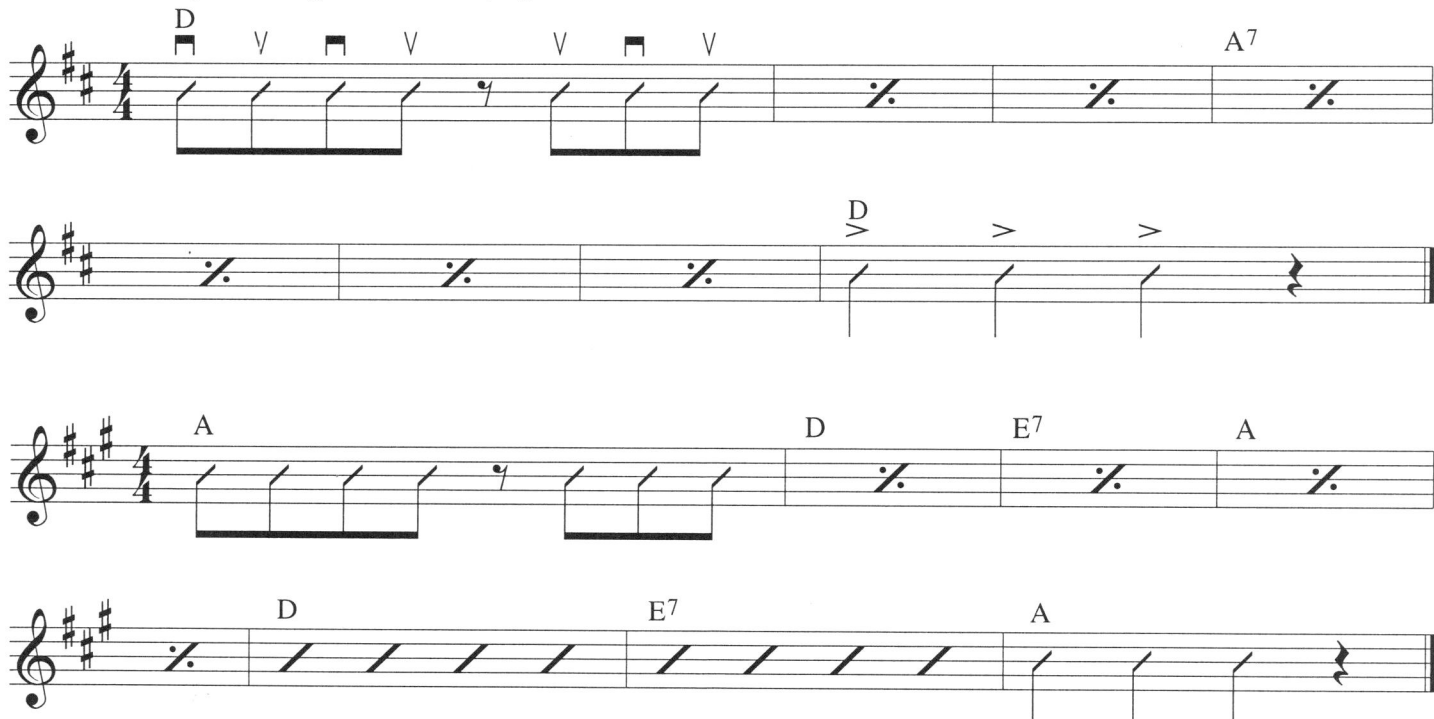

Occasionally the chord must be changed in the middle of a measure. When this happens, change on the "and" of 2, as in the example below:

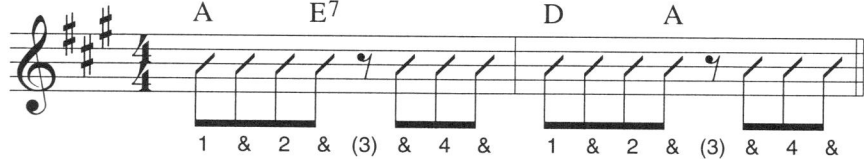

Hey Lolly Lolly

(Student to learn both the strum and solo parts)

Traditional calypso song

Hey lol - ly, lol - ly lol - ly, hey lol - ly, lol - ly lo,—
Hey lol - ly, lol - ly lol - ly, hey lol - ly, lol - ly lo.— *Fine*
First you sing— a sim - ple line,— hey lol - ly, lol - ly lo,—
Then you try— and make it rhyme,— hey lol - ly, lol - ly lo.— *D.C. al Fine*

The Sloop "John B."

Calypso tempo

Introduction

Traditional calypso song

So hoist up the John B. sails, see how the main sail set, send for the cap - tain a - shore let— me go home.— Oh, let— me go home,— please let— me go home, I feel so break— up, I wan - na go home.

The Key of D Minor

As you have already learned, the key signature of one flat signifies the key of F major. It can also indicate the key of D minor which is called the relative minor key of F major. The one flat in the key signature means that all B's are played as B♭ unless preceded by a natural sign.

Here are three different D minor scales. Follow the fingering carefully and add them to your daily practice routine.

The D Natural Minor Scale

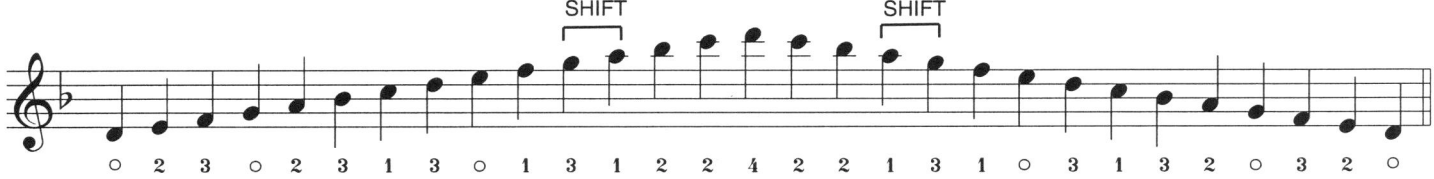

The D Harmonic Minor Scale

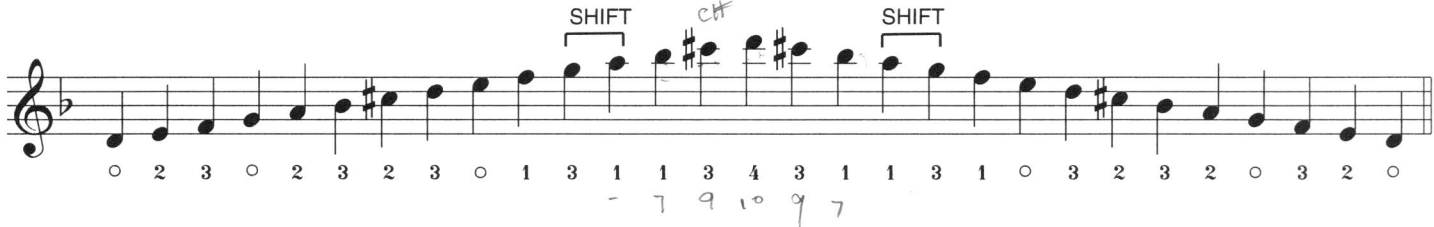

The D Melodic Minor Scale

(Notice that when this scale descends the 6th and 7th notes of the scale are lowered a half step.)

The Three Principal Chords in D Minor with Bass Notes

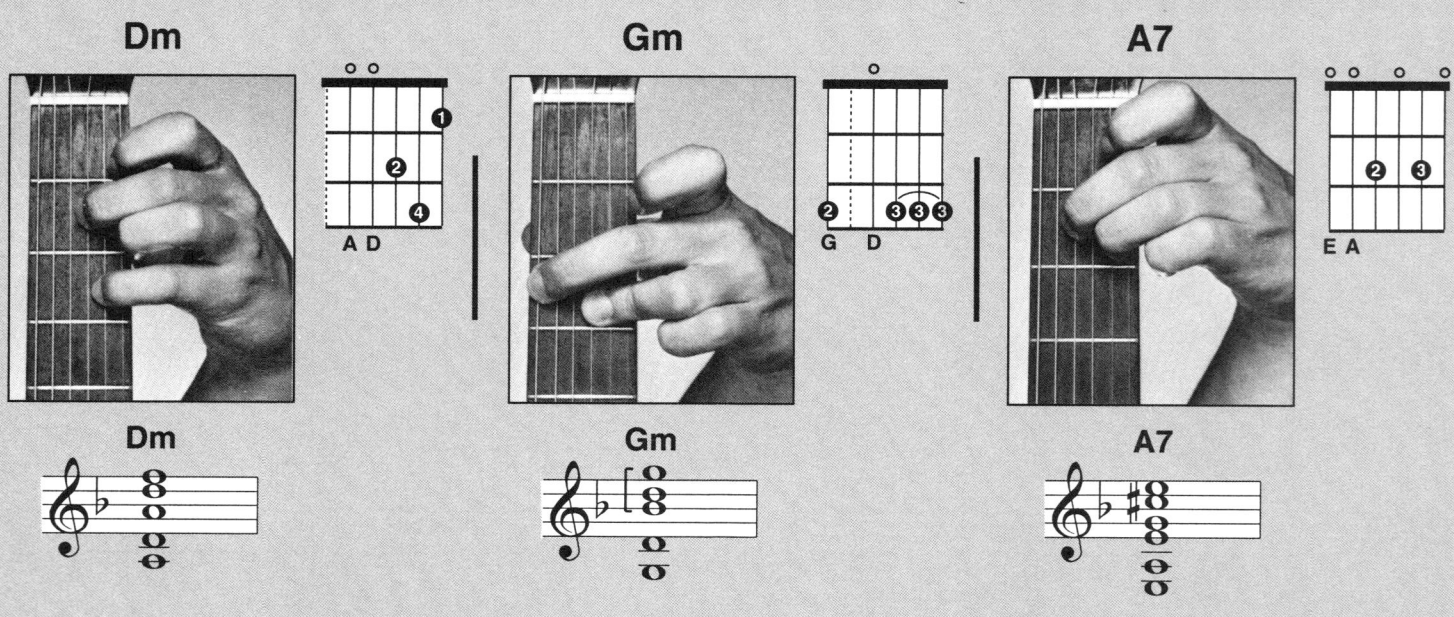

Sicilian Tarantella

A tarantella is a dance of Italian origin that supposedly mimics the movements of someone who has been bitten by a tarantula. This tarantella is very popular and is often performed at Italian weddings.

Sixteenth Notes and 6/8 Time

As in 2/4, 3/4 and 4/4 time, in 6/8 time sixteenth notes are played twice as fast as eighth notes. Compare the following:

The old folk song "House of the Rising Sun" became a big hit in the '60s using this accompaniment in 6/8 time. This accompaniment may be used with the arrangement of "House of the Rising Sun" on the facing page. (Hold chords as much as possible.)

The House of the Rising Sun

(Duet in E Minor—student to learn both parts)

Traditional

HOLD CHORDS WHEREVER POSSIBLE

The Key of E Major

The key signature of four sharps indicates the key of E major. Although at first the student may find the number of sharps confusing, it is well worth the effort to master this key, because it is the key in which the guitar sounds best. Many of the best-known blues, country, folk and rock songs are in the key of E for this reason.

The key signature of four sharps means that all F's are played as F#, all C's are played as C#, all G's are played as G# and all D's are played as D#. That is, all the sharps in the key of A plus D#.

When learning the two-octave E major scale below, follow the fingering carefully. Like all scales this one should be practiced daily.

The Three Principal Chords in E with Bass Notes

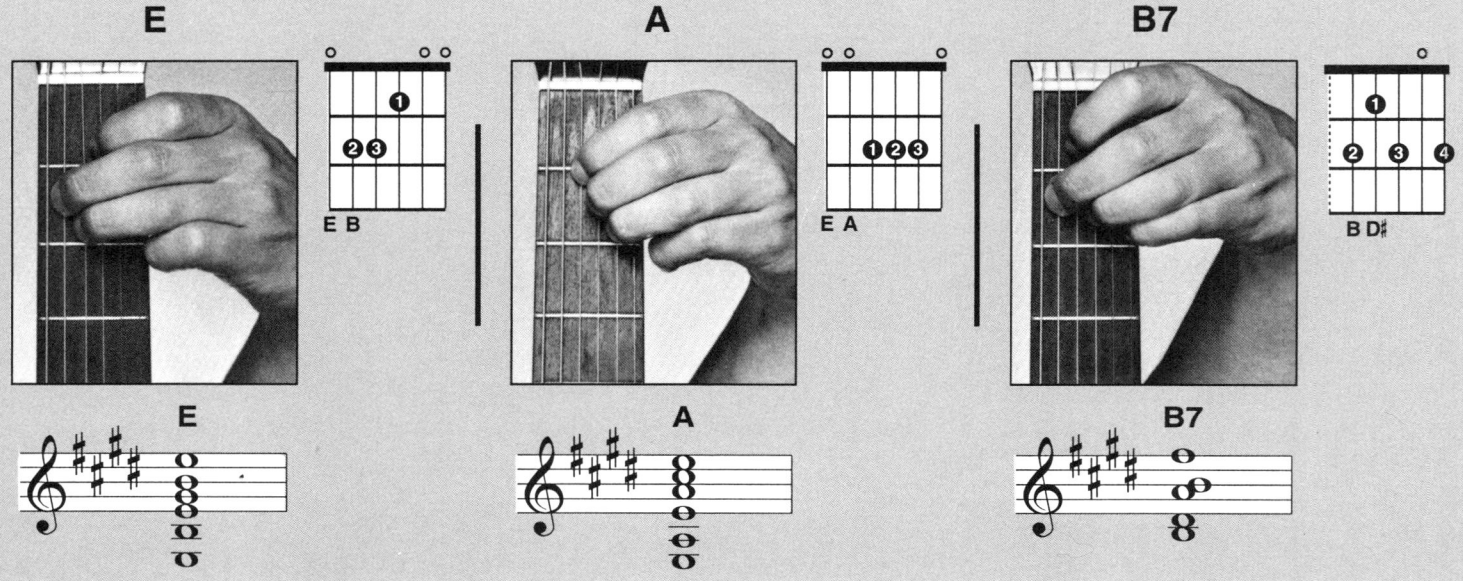

Accompaniments in E Major

Finger Exercise in E

A valuable exercise for the 2nd and 4th fingers. Remember that F, C, G and D are sharp.

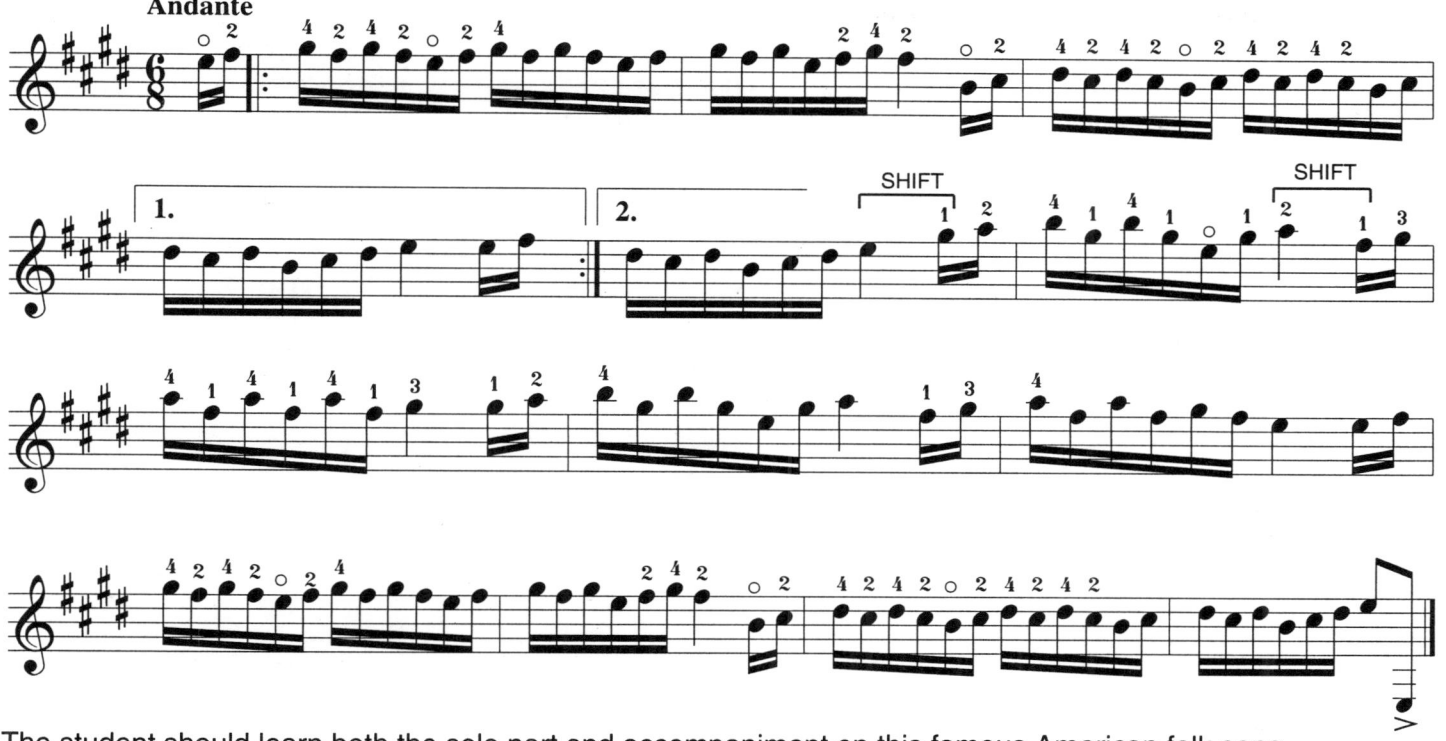

The student should learn both the solo part and accompaniment on this famous American folk song.

The Blue Tail Fly

In part 1, called the verse, each chord should be strummed once where it appears. Tempo is free in this part.

In part 2, called the chorus or refrain, play a perky bass/chord accompaniment similar to the one in 2/4 time on the preceding page.

* This mark (//) is called a caesura in classical music. Pop musicians call them railroad tracks. They mean to leave an extra pause between the two notes.

Using Passing Notes in the Bass

As you have learned on previous pages, the bass/chord style of accompaniment is generally more effective than just strumming a chord on each beat. The bass notes used are the root (or name of the chord), the 5th and sometimes the 3rd of the chord. The chart below shows the various choices of bass note for every chord that you've learned.

Name of Chord	Root	5th	3rd
C	C	G	E
C7	C	G	E
F	F	C	A
G	G	D	B
G7	G	D	B
G minor	G	D	B♭
D	D	A	F♯
D7	D	A	F♯
D minor	D	A	F
A	A	E	C♯
A7	A	E	C♯
A minor	A	E	C
E	E	B	G♯
E7	E	B	G♯
E minor	E	B	G
B7	B	F♯	D♯

Generally the root should be your first choice, although when playing 7th chords it is often more effective to use an alternate note first. Your second choice can be dictated by how easy it is to get to it. For example, the note E in a C chord is the 3rd of that chord; it is easier to get to than the 5th (the note G).

Using Passing Notes in the Bass (cont'd.)

It is sometimes effective to use passing notes to connect the ordinary bass notes of a chord. Passing notes are notes that do not belong to the chord, but connect the notes that do belong to it (the root, 5th or 3rd) usually by step. Here are some examples of various styles.

Diminished Chords

So far all the chords you have learned belong to three different families: major, minor and seventh. Another type of chord common in jazz, classical and pop music is the diminished chord. Diminished chords can be derived from ordinary 7th chords **by flatting every note in the 7th chord except the root**.

For example, starting with D7, we have the notes D (root), F♯ (3rd), A (5th) and C (7th).

D7
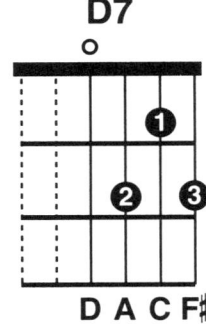
D A C F♯

To make a D7 into a D diminished chord, flat the 3rd, 5th, and 7th a half step or one fret. This gives us the notes D, F A♭, and C♭ (or B).

D dim.
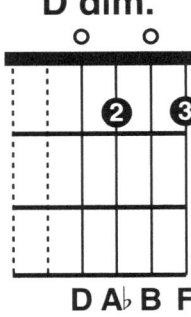
D A♭ B F

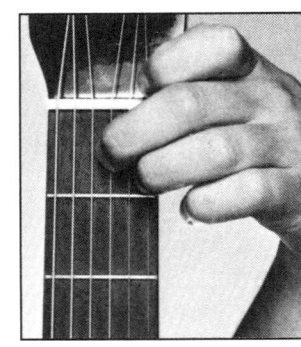

Starting with A7, we have A (root), C♯ (3rd), E (5th) and G (7th).

A7
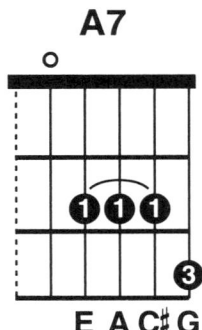
E A C♯ G

To make an A7 into an A diminished chord, flat the 3rd, 5th, and 7th a half step. This gives us the notes A, C, E♭, and G♭ (or F♯).

A dim.
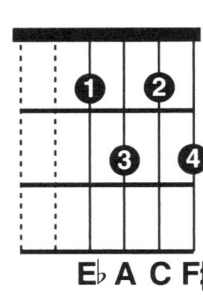
E♭ A C F♯

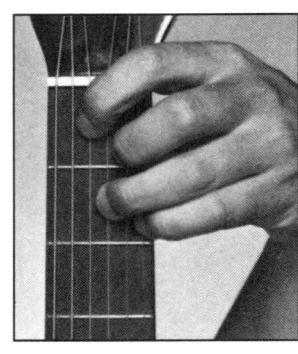

Starting with E7, we have E (root), G♯ (3rd), B (5th) and D (7th).

E7
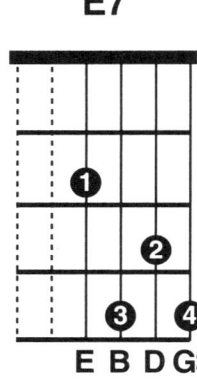
E B D G♯

To make an E7 into an E diminished chord, flat the 3rd, 5th, and 7th a half step. This gives us the notes E, G, B♭, and D♭ (or C♯).

E dim.
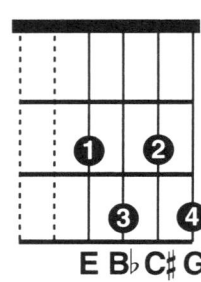
E B♭ C♯ G

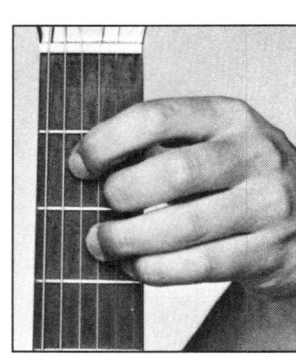

The good news is that these three diminished chords can be used for every diminished chord in music:

D dim. = F dim. = A♭ or G♯ dim. = B dim.

A dim. = C dim. = E♭ or D♯ dim. = G♭ or F♯ dim.

E dim. = G dim. = B♭ dim. = D♭ or C♯ dim.

For a bass note, pick any low note in the diminished chord that moves smoothly to your next bass note.

You Tell Me Your Dream

(Solo with Diminished Chords)

Pull-offs

The pull-off effect is very common in all types of music, but especially in rock, heavy metal, country, blues and jazz. Like the hammer-on (see page 16), the pull-off allows you to play a note without using the right hand.

A pull-off to a *fingered* string is done like this:

1. Start with a fingered note, the G on the 1st string, 3rd fret.

2. Pick the 1st string with the 1st and 3rd fingers on F and G.

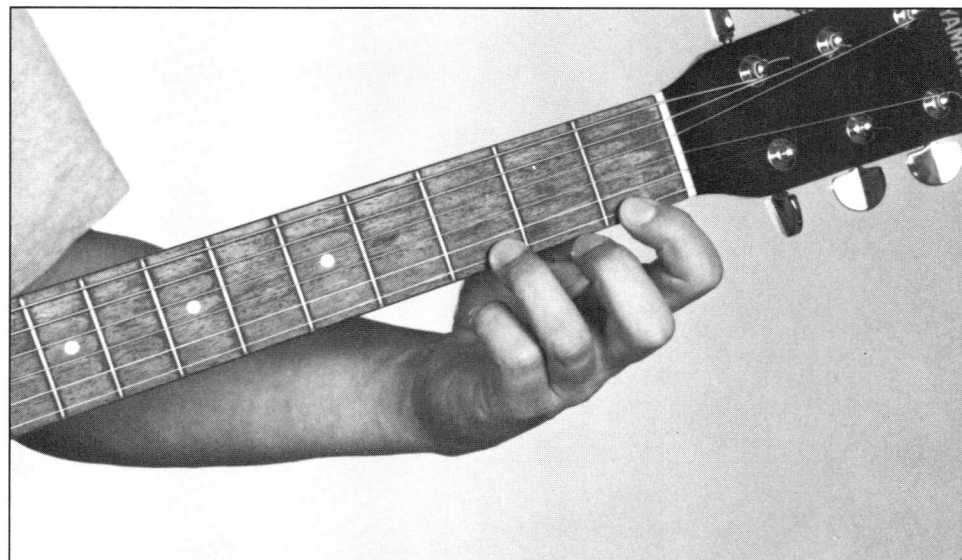

3. Pull the 3rd finger off the string with a lateral motion so that the F sounds clearly.

In musical notation, this is written:

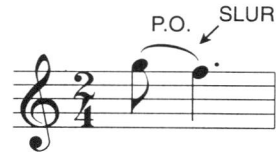

The curved line between the G and the F is a slur which means that the F is not picked. The initials P.O. stand for pull-off, but not all publications use this notation.

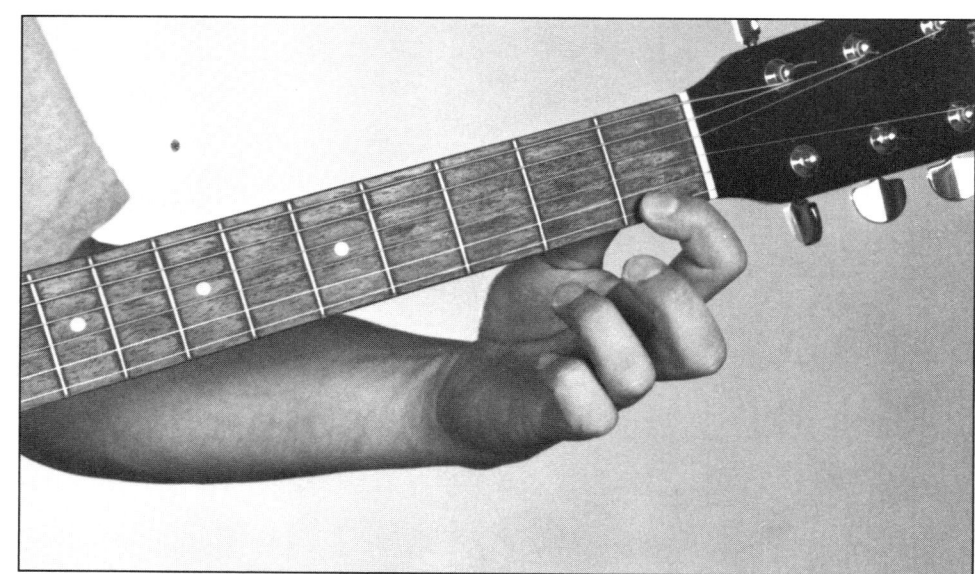

A pull-off to an *open* string is done like this:

1. Start with a fingered note, as an example, the G on the 1st string, 3rd fret.

2. Pick the 1st string with the 3rd finger on G.

3. Pull the 3rd finger off the string using a lateral motion so that the open E sounds clearly.

Here it is in music notation:

The Polka

As its name implies, the polka was originally a Polish dance. It was brought to the United States in the 19th century and still enjoys great popularity. Polka albums are always among the top sellers regardless of other trends that may be popular. This polka is based on the folk song "Little Brown Jug."

33

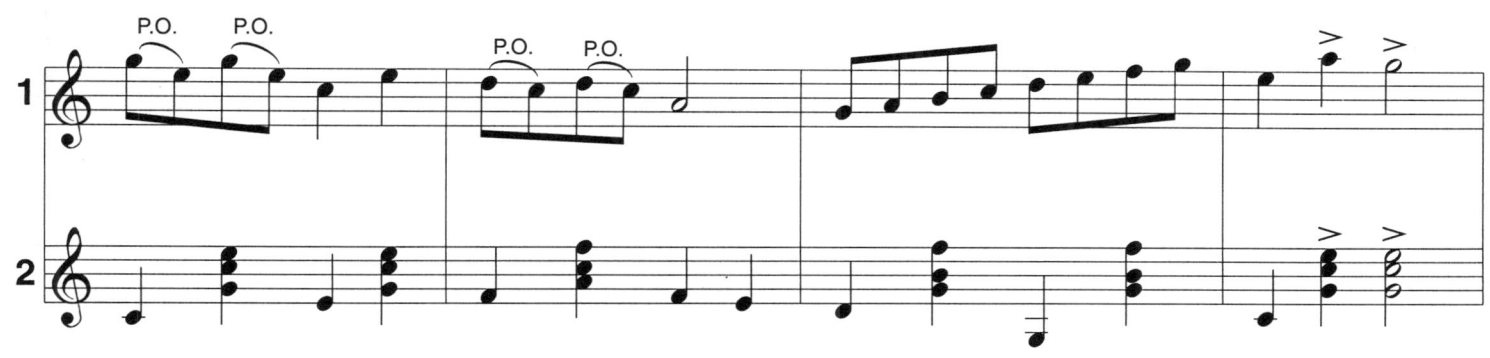

Grace Notes

A grace note is a small note (usually an 8th note) with a slash mark through the flag placed before a normal-sized note, like this:

The grace note is played very light and fast (not accented) just before the regular note.

On the guitar, grace notes are played three different ways:

1. From below, as a quick hammer-on using two fingers

2. From above, as a quick pull-off using two fingers

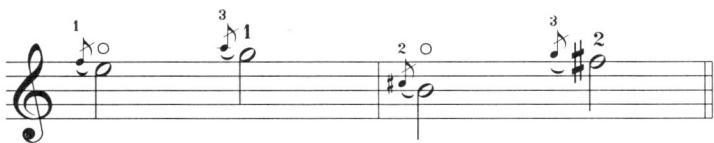

3. From either below or above, as a quick slide (see page 38) from the grace note to the regular note using one finger

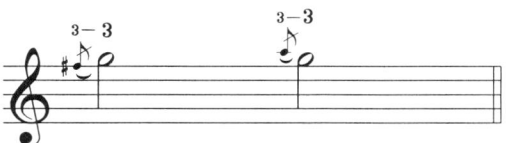

Grace notes can be very effective in adding sparkle to a melody, and guitarists like them because they sound good and are easy to play. Although it would be possible to play grace notes before every note in a melody, this would soon become an irritating mannerism, and the tasteful player will limit the use of grace notes to a few effective places.

Amazing Grace Notes

In the following study play the grace notes whichever way is most comfortable and the way they sound best to you.

Colonel Bogey

This great march became popular after its use in the movie classic "The Bridge on the River Kwai." Follow the fingering carefully on the grace notes.

Kenneth J. Alford

March

NOTE: E♯ IS THE SAME AS F♮, 1st STRING, 1st FRET

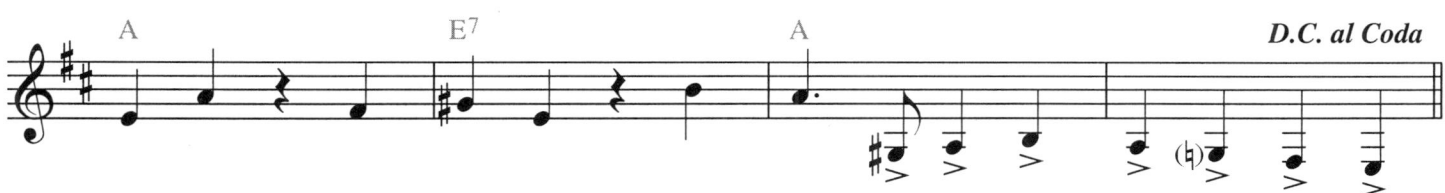

Coda

Augmented Chords

To augment something means to make it larger. In music, an augmented chord is one in which the interval from the root to the 5th has been made larger by a half step.

C Major

For example, starting with the C major chord, we have the notes C (root), E (3rd) and G (5th).

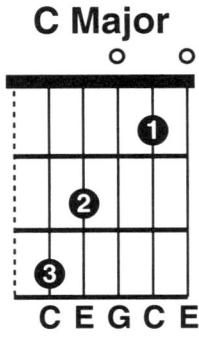

C E G C E

C Aug

To make a C major chord into a C augmented chord, raise the 5th a half step, to G♯.

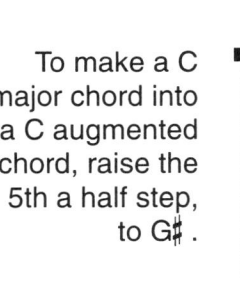

C E G♯ C E

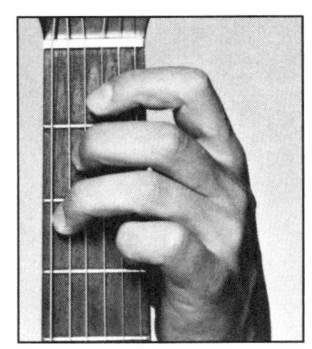

G Major

Starting with a G major chord, we have G (root), B (3rd) and D (5th).

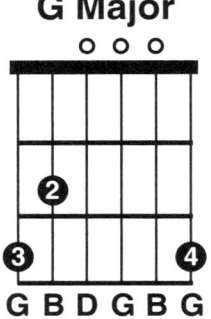

G B D G B G

G Aug

To make a G major chord into a G augmented chord, raise the 5th a half step, to D♯.

G B D♯ G B G

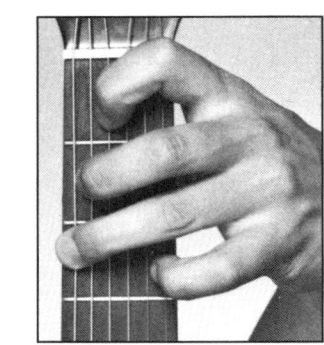

F Major

Starting with an F major chord, we have F (root), A (3rd) and C (5th).

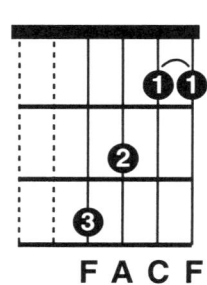

F A C F

F Aug

To make an F major chord into an F augmented chord, raise the 5th a half step, to C♯.

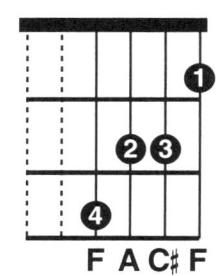

F A C♯ F

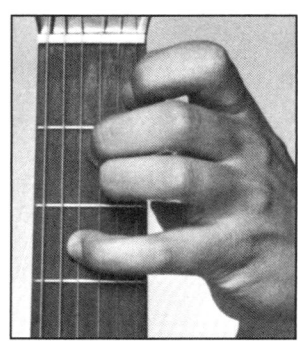

D Major

Starting with a D major chord, we have D (root), F♯ (3rd) and A (5th).

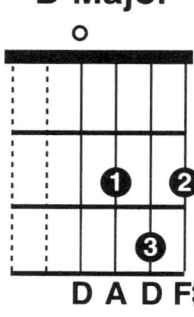

D A D F♯

D Aug

To make a D major chord into a D augmented chord, raise the 5th a half step, to A♯.

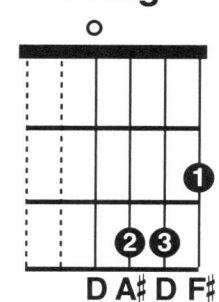

D A♯ D F♯

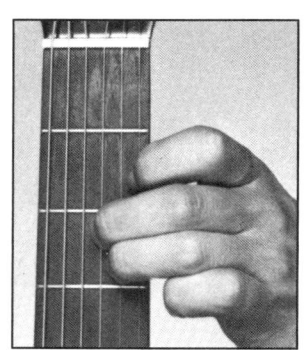

The good news is that these four chords can be used for every augmented chord in music:

C augmented	=	E augmented	=	G♯ or A♭ augmented
G augmented	=	B augmented	=	D♯ or E♭ augmented
F augmented	=	A augmented	=	C♯ or D♭ augmented
D augmented	=	F♯ augmented	=	A♯ or B♭ augmented

Augmented Chords (cont'd.)

Augmented chords are almost unknown in rock, blues and folk music, but are greatly used in jazz and pop songs prior to the rock era. The following chord progressions are typical of the way augmented chords are used.

IMPORTANT: In modern sheet music, augmented chords are usually indicated by a plus sign (for example C+, G+ and so on).

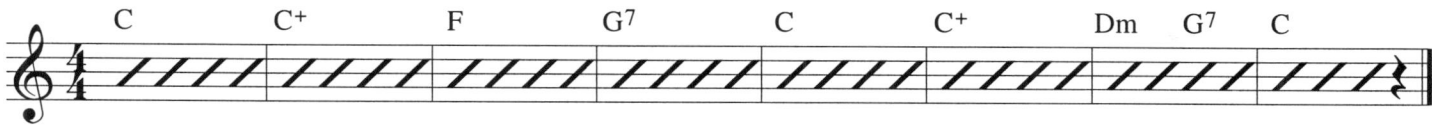

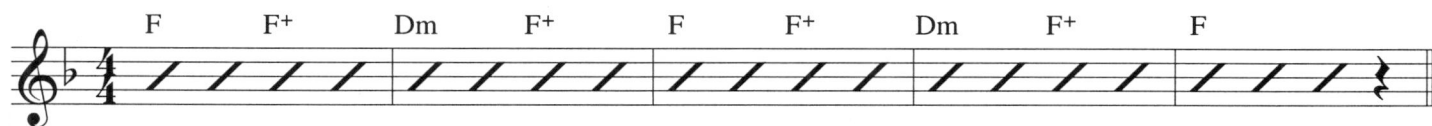

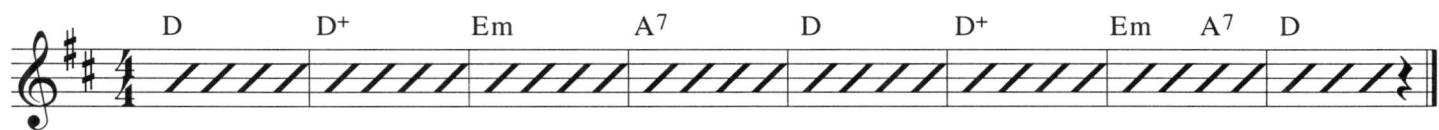

The following chord progression fits the melody of the great Duke Ellington standard *Take the A Train*. Note the extensive use of augmented chords.

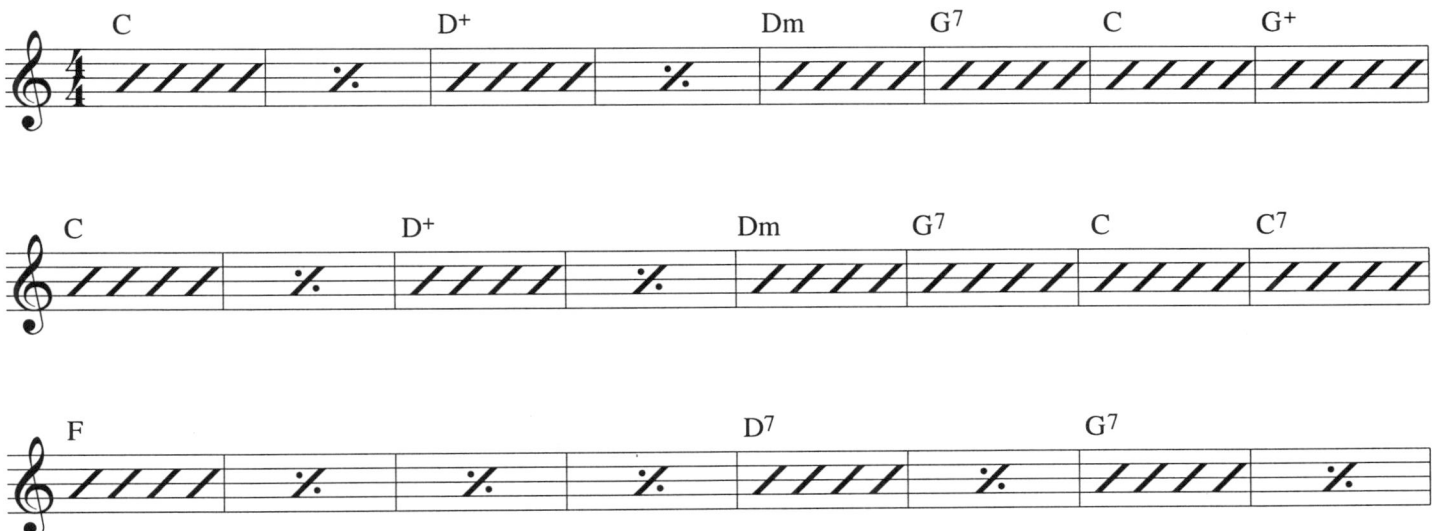

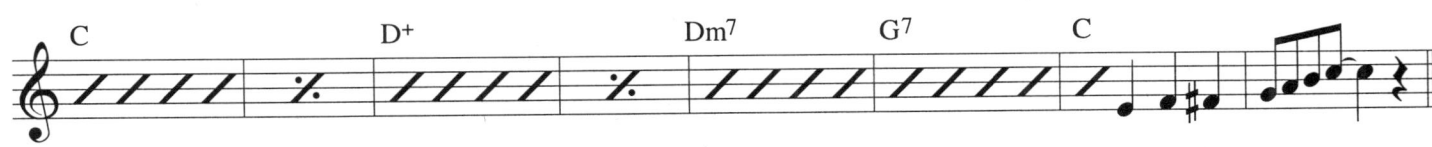

Slides and How To Play Them

Sliding up to or away from a note is an effective device that is much used by today's guitar players.

1. Sliding from one note to another. This must always be done on one string, either up or down. Finger the first note and pick the string. Then, without releasing the pressure on the string, slide to the next note.

   In musical notation:

   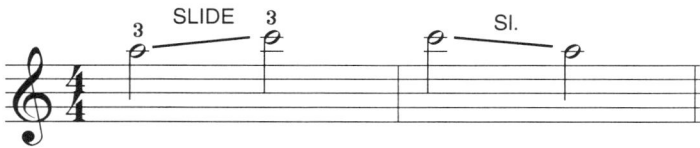

2. Often the slide begins on an indefinite note a few frets above or below the final note. Start with a little pressure on the string, but not enough to press it down to the fret. Then, as you slide toward the final note, gradually increase the pressure so that when you reach the final note it sounds clear.

   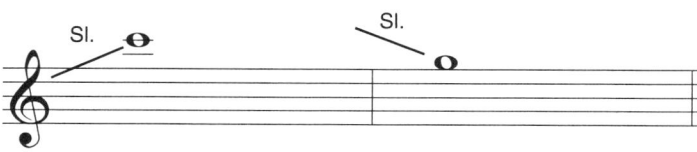

3. Sliding away from a definite note to an indefinite note is more or less the reverse of #2 above. Start with any note that is at least five frets up the fingerboard. Pick the string, and as you slide down and away from the note, gradually release the pressure on the string so that your finger stops its vibration.

   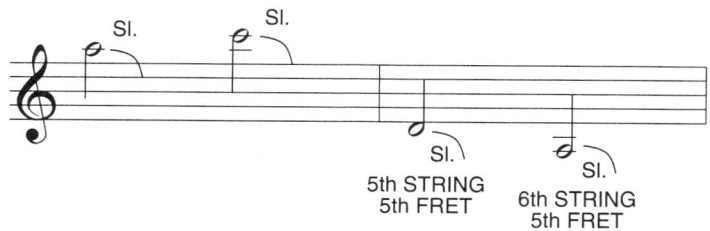

Slidin' Around

This duet demonstrates the use of slides in blues playing. For best results, the student should learn both parts. If playing alone, play the 2nd part first, then the 1st part, then the 2nd part again to finish up. If playing as a duet, have the 2nd player play the arrangement through once, then add the top part. More advanced players will want to improvise some blues against the funky bass line.

Tunes that Teach Technic No. 2

*An oberek (o-BED-ek) is a lively Polish dance popular with the same people that enjoys polkas.

Abide with Me

This arrangement of the lovely old hymn combines a chord/melody solo in the 1st part with an arpeggio-style accompaniment in the 2nd part. The student should learn both parts. Also note that the accompaniment is always played at a dynamic one level lower than the melody part.

Words by Henry Francis Lyte

Music by William H. Monk

HOLD FINGERS DOWN AS LONG AS POSSIBLE

*Lento means to play slowly.

Beguine
(be-GEEN)

The beguine is a graceful dance of Afro-Cuban origin which became known in the U.S. about 1930, and which has remained popular ever since. Its rhythm makes ingenious use of the bass/chord style on guitar, breaking up the bass notes and the chords in a syncopated pattern that gives the dance its characteristic sound.

The basic rhythm of the beguine is:

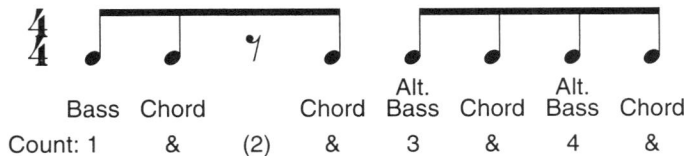

Notice that the pattern is simply a bass/chord pattern played in eighth notes, *but with the second bass note omitted*. It is this omission of the second downbeat that gives the rhythm of the beguine its characteristic sound.

First practice the beguine rhythm on the D and A7 chords as written out below. Then learn both the melody and the accompaniment of the beautiful Italian beguine "Guitarra Romana" (Roman Guitar).

Guitarra Romana
(Roman Guitar)

Eldo di Lazzaro

Copyright © MCMXXXVII by Alfred Publishing Co., Inc.

For a very nice effect during the following interlude, solo guitar can lightly muffle the strings with the "heel" of the right hand. This produces a sound like that of pizzicato strings.

Bends or Chokes

The laws of acoustics state that when the tension of a string is increased, its pitch rises. Blues players discovered this at least a hundred years ago, and the technic now called "bending" or "choking" a string has become a standard part of the modern guitarist's bag of tricks. Here's how to do it:

1. Finger any note on any of the first five strings and pick the string. Take, for example, the note E on the 2nd string, 5th fret.

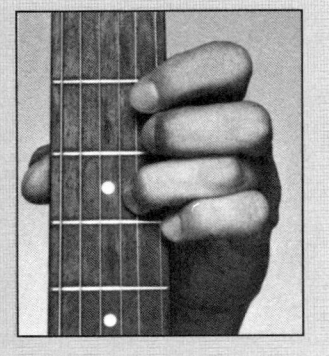

2. Keeping the pressure on the string, push it across the fingerboard till you hear the pitch rise a half step, from E to F

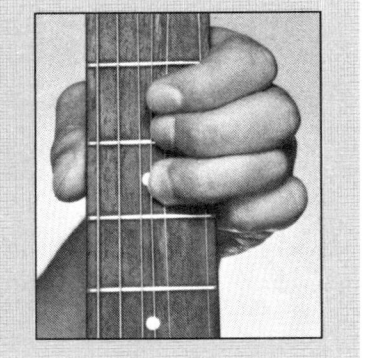

Bends do not work too well on the lower frets, so make sure the note you're bending is at least on the 3rd fret or higher. Also make sure you're using a light-gauge string. It's difficult to do this effect if the string is too stiff.

Modern heavy metal players often bend notes a whole step, 1-1/2 steps and even 2 steps higher. This can be accomplished by using an extremely light gauge string—.008s—and playing up around the 12th fret.

When bending notes on the low E, the string must be *pulled* to avoid pushing it off the fingerboard.

Playing A on the 6th string, 5th fret.

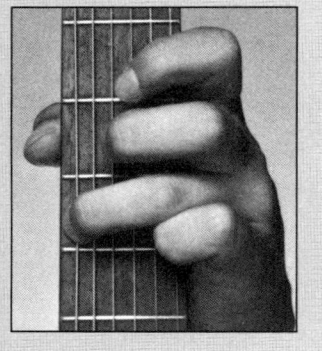

Bending A to an A♯

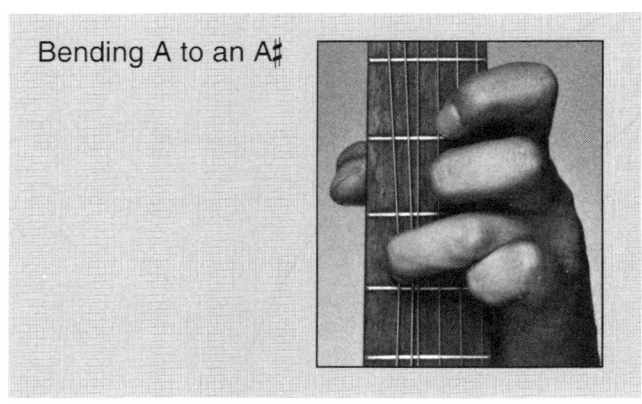

Unfortunately for the student, the notation of this effect is still in contention. Some arrangers write the *fingered* note and indicate by using an arrow that it should be bent up a 1/2 step or more. Others prefer to write the *final* pitch with a notation to bend it up from a lower note. In this book we use the former notation.

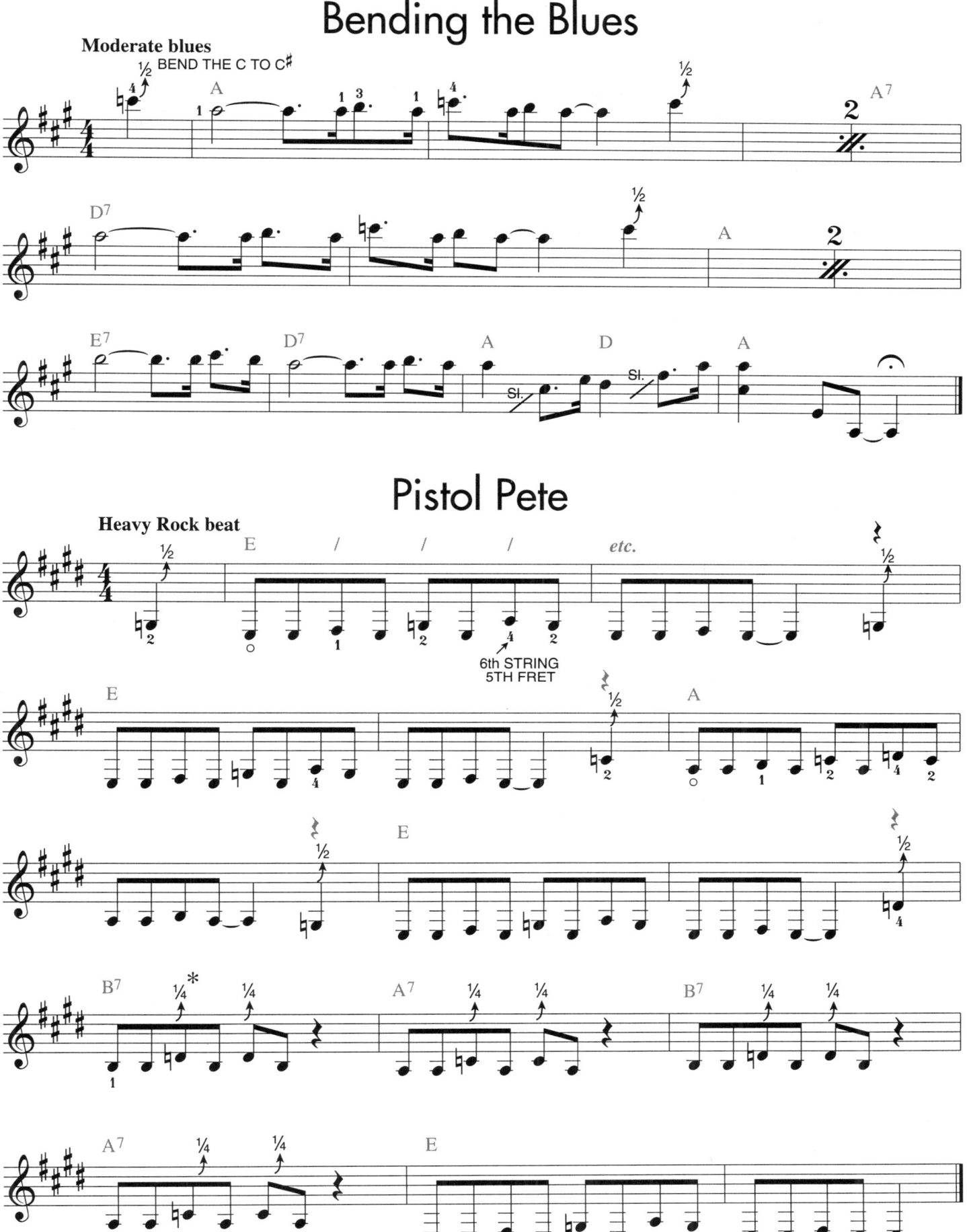

* The arrow with 1/4 above it is often used to mean: Pull the note up a quarter of a step, that is, not quite up to the next note. One advantage that guitar players have over piano players is that they can play these sounds that do not exist on a piano.

Counterpoint

The word "counterpoint" means playing two or more melodies at the same time. Of course, the idea is that they sound good together. In classical music the unquestioned master of counterpoint was the great J.S. Bach (1685–1750) who thought nothing of *improvising* four- and five-part fugues. Counterpoint hasn't been used much in popular music, but occasionally a little gem turns up, like *Simple Melody* by Irving Berlin.

In this one, he manages to write two different melodies that sound good individually or when played simultaneously. The following arrangement can be played in several ways. Either of the parts marked 1 and 2 can be played as a solo or as a solo accompanied by part 3. Or, all three parts can be played simultaneously.

Simple Melody

Words and Music by Irving Berlin

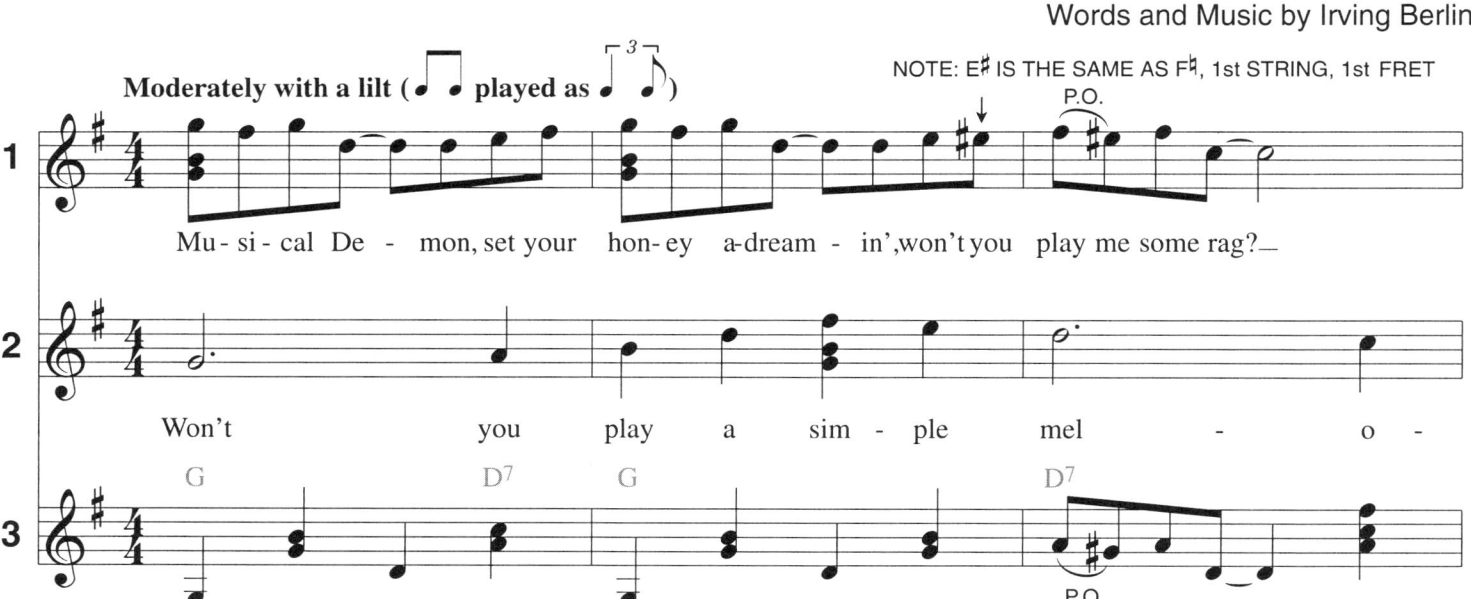

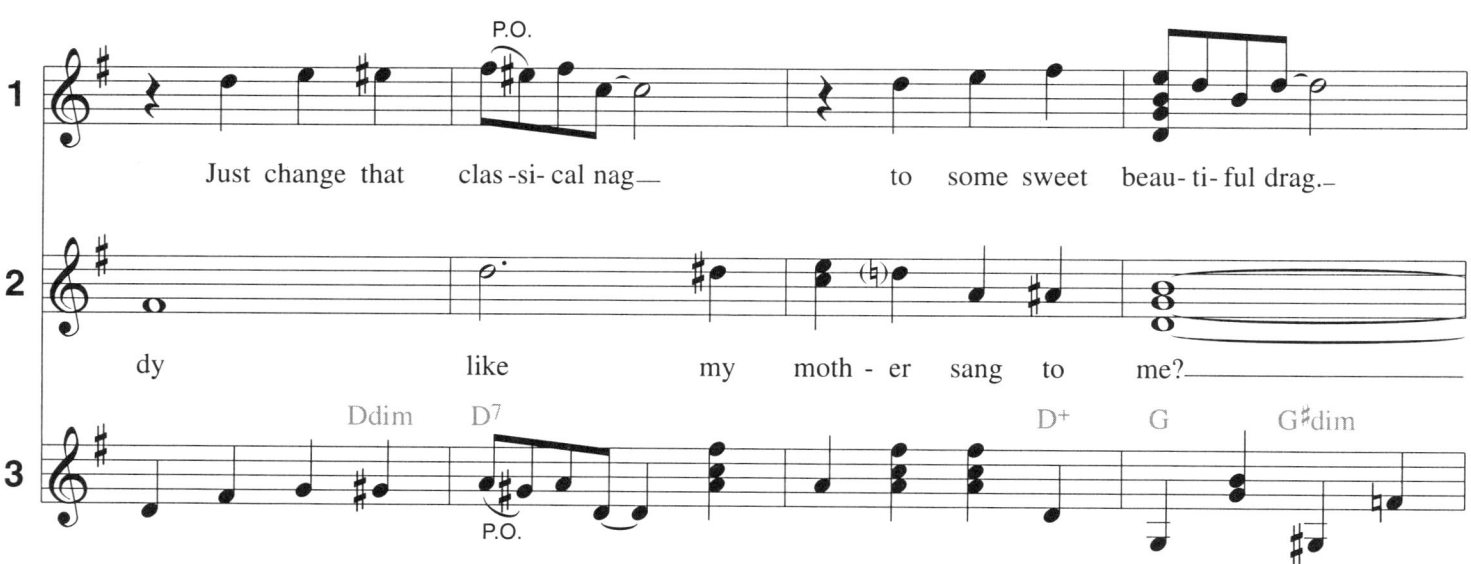

Tunes That Teach Technic No. 3

The last technique described in this book combines pull offs and hammer ons in ways that are used by today's hottest rock, blues and jazz guitarists. Concentrate on articulating clearly. That is, make sure each note sounds clear regardless of whether or not it is picked.

Onyx Club Hop

Just Lopin' Along

Jingle for a Sunny Day